SO YOU WANT TO BE BLESSED:

A Devotional Commentary

of Psalm One

by

Darin Bowler

Note for Librarians: A cataloguing record for this book is available from Library and
Archives Canada at www.collectionscanada.ca/amicus/index-e.html
ISBN 1-4120-6008-7

*Printed in Victoria, BC, Canada. Printed on paper with minimum 30% recycled fibre. Trafford's print
shop runs on "green energy" from solar, wind and other environmentally-friendly power sources.*

TRAFFORD™
PUBLISHING

Offices in Canada, USA, Ireland and UK
This book was published *on-demand* in cooperation with Trafford Publishing.
On-demand publishing is a unique process and service of making a book available for
retail sale to the public taking advantage of on-demand manufacturing and Internet
marketing. On-demand publishing includes promotions, retail sales, manufacturing,
order fulfilment, accounting and collecting royalties on behalf of the author.

Book sales for North America and international:
Trafford Publishing, 6E–2333 Government St.,
Victoria, BC v8t 4p4 CANADA
phone 250 383 6864 (toll-free 1 888 232 4444)
fax 250 383 6804; email to orders@trafford.com
Book sales in Europe:
Trafford Publishing (uk) Limited, 9 Park End Street, 2nd Floor
Oxford, UK ox1 1hh UNITED KINGDOM
phone 44 (0)1865 722 113 (local rate 0845 230 9601)
facsimile 44 (0)1865 722 868; info.uk@trafford.com
Order online at:
trafford.com/05-0909

10 9 8 7 6 5 4 3 2

To my father,
Roland Bowler.

Blessed is the man that walketh not in the counsel of the ungodly, nor standeth in the way of sinners, nor sitteth in the seat of the scornful. But his delight is in the law of the LORD; and in his law doth he meditate day and night. And he shall be like a tree planted by the rivers of water, that bringeth forth his fruit in his season; his leaf also shall not wither; and whatsoever he doeth shall prosper. The ungodly are not so: but are like the chaff which the wind driveth away. Therefore the ungodly shall not stand in the judgment, nor sinners in the congregation of the righteous. For the LORD knoweth the way of the righteous: but the way of the ungodly shall perish.

(Psalm One)

"Blessed is the man that walketh not in the counsel of the ungodly..."

CHAPTER ONE

In 1874 a precious commodity was discovered in the Black Hills of Dakota~something called gold. Normally that would have been a good thing for the United States: more wealth, more power, more affluence and stability. But there was one problem. Six years earlier the Sioux Indians had been guaranteed ownership of the Black Hills. The U.S. government offered to purchase the territory, but the Sioux Indians refused to sell. So the U.S. government gave an ultimatum: get out or be driven out. The ultimatum was ignored, so the war department was authorized to commence operations against noncompliant Sioux Indians. A plan was devised whereby one thousand troops of U.S. soldiers would surround and destroy the Sioux Indians. Col. George Custer of the Seventh Cavalry was ordered to wait for backup troops to arrive in order to assist him in his attack. Colonel Custer disobeyed orders and with only 365 men he initiated an attack on Chief Sitting Bull's village. On June 25, 1876 Colonel Custer and his men were violently massacred by two thousand

Sioux warriors. This became known as the Battle of Little Big Horn. It is commonly recognized as one of the worst battle defeats ever suffered by U.S. forces. Because Col. George Custer refused to heed the counsel of his superiors there was a loss of many lives.

In a similar parallel there are many lives today that are in disarray and shambles because of a failure to heed biblical counsel. Many of the troubling situations that people find themselves in are because of either a failure or a refusal to heed biblical directives. Often people will worsen and prolong their dire situations because they consistently rely upon earthly wisdom and man-made philosophies to guide them through life. Paul stated:

For the wisdom of this world is foolishness with God... (I Corinthians 3:19)

Proverbs 14:12 tells us, "There is a way which seemeth right unto a man, but the end thereof are the ways of death." Combine that with "for my thoughts are not your thoughts, neither are your ways my ways, saith the Lord. For as the heavens are higher than the earth, so are my ways higher than your ways, and my thoughts than your thoughts" (Isaiah 55:8,9). Add to that, "the carnal mind is enmity against God" (Romans 8:7). When considering all of these factors it becomes apparent that the natural mind is in no condition to comprehend the ways of God. Because of the limited condition of our minds we are susceptible to error and false judgment. In spite of all of our scientific discoveries and technological breakthroughs, there remains a dimension that our natural minds can never completely fathom ~ the wisdom of God. The first characteristic of the blessed man is his refusal to walk in the counsel of the ungodly. Fortune-telling gurus, psychics and advisors who do not build their ideas and philosophies upon the unchangeable principles of God's Word are not the safest individuals to submit to when facing the dilemmas, hard choices and battles of life. They (like Colonel Custer) are ill-equipped and unqualified to safely lead God-fearing souls to spiritual health. Peter instructed us to "gird up the loins of your mind" (I Peter 1:13) . That means to protect your mind and guard it.

Not only are we vulnerable to humanistic philosophies, but we are vulnerable to spiritual influences as well. In Ephesians 6 the apostle Paul wrote these words to describe the spiritual powers that are at work in our world:

We wrestle not against flesh and blood, but against principalities, against powers, against the rulers of the darkness of this world, against spiritual wickedness in high places. Wherefore take unto you the whole armor of God, that ye may be able to withstand in the evil day, and having done all, to stand. Stand therefore having your loins girt about with truth, and having on the breastplate of righteousness; and your feet shod with the preparation of the gospel of peace; above all, taking the shield of faith, wherewith ye shall be able to quench all the fiery darts of the wicked. And take the helmet of salvation, and the sword of the Spirit, which is the word of God: praying always with all prayer and supplication in the Spirit, and watching thereunto with all perseverance and supplication for all saints (Ephesians 6:12-18).

This passage helps us to understand the fact that some of the things we contend with in this world are spiritual in nature. In Ephesians 2 Paul wrote:

And you hath he quickened, who were dead in trespasses and sins; wherein in time past ye walked according to the course of this world, according to the prince of the power of the air, the spirit that now worketh in the children of disobedience (Ephesians 2:1-2).

From these passages of scripture alone it is obvious that spiritual wickedness is real. There are unseen forces that war against the kingdom of God. While not all of the problems we contend with are necessarily spiritual in nature I do believe we might be surprised at how much is actually influenced by spiritual activity.

Paul mentioned spiritual wickedness existing in "high places." This refers to a certain degree of spiritual activity occurring within places of great power and influence. The first main area that comes to mind is government. In government there are many individuals who carry great influence. There are governors, congressmen, senators, lawmakers and decision-makers that with one stroke of the pen have the ability to affect the lives of millions of individuals.

Another area of high influence is within our institutions of education. Never underestimate the power of a teacher. As a young man I was raised in a good home with Christian parents. They taught me and reared me well. But the one person that I would specifically thank for influencing me to never take drugs would be a Sunday school teacher by the name of Lucy Castro. When I was a boy of about five years old in Sunday school class Sister Castro looked me right in the eye and said, "Don't ever take drugs. They TWIST your brain!" Now at five years old I barely even knew what a brain was. But one thing was for sure, I didn't want it twisted! I said, "They twist your brain?!" "Yes," she replied, "they twist your brain!" That day I made up my mind that I would never take drugs a day in my life. Several years later a young man held a smoking marijuana joint in front of my face and offered for me to take a "hit." Sister Castro's face flashed into my mind and I remembered her words. I refused. Teachers can have a profound influence on the lives of others. Because of that I believe that one area of high prominence and influence is within our institutions of education, especially colleges and universities. In these classrooms are perhaps some of the most ambitious and potential-laden people in the entire world. If these young minds can be shaped and influenced toward ungodly principles and values you can be sure that will be a place of highly concentrated spiritual activity as well.

Another "high place" I believe lies within the areas of the media and the entertainment industry. Here again there are highly influential people that are seen and admired by millions of star-struck fans~writers and producers and directors that labor to entertain the masses. If just one writer can be influenced to weave into his scripts and characters ungodly ideas and immoral philosophies and then present them in a positive light, he can easily influence millions of young and impressionable minds. For instance, just let the star of a TV program or film be attractive, funny and well liked. And occasionally have this character verbally endorse unbiblical principles and there will be in an instant millions of individuals gradually leaning toward the same ideologies. The entertainment industry is most certainly an area of highly focused spiritual activity.

I personally can attest to the influential power of the media. In the very early nineties I was just beginning to grow in my calling to ministry. At this particular time in my life I wasn't much of a follower of political affairs. But one thing that I was convinced of was that our then vice president Dan Quayle was an inept buffoon. Why did I believe that? Because of the media. At that time Dan Quayle was the subject of many insulting jokes and remarks. I simply and blindly followed the crowd. But one night I was made aware of an article concerning the convictions that Dan Quayle stood by. I was shocked at the Christian morals and principles that he defended. It suddenly dawned on me that I had been duped and blindsided by the spirit of antichrist that reigns in the media!

The Bible also mentions "doctrines of devils." Apparently there are even some teachings that originate in spiritual wickedness (see I Timothy 4:1). Paul also warned about philosophies that are "not after Christ" (Colossians 2:8). By just observing these few scriptures it is obvious that there is an onslaught of many ungodly influences at work in our world. We know that there is an abandoning of godly, time-proven principles taking place in our nation. Many of them are principles upon which this nation was founded. The time would fail to tell of the many magazines, self-help books, horoscopes and newspaper articles that further spread these unbiblical theories and philosophies. Many of them are designed to improve our lives and to help us solve our problems. Most of them may sound appealing to our carnal nature, but the true child of God will always endeavor to adhere to biblical guidance and counsel.

In Daniel 7:9 God is referred to as the "Ancient of Days." (That means He's been around a pretty long time). The truth is God knows and understands more than you or I. He knows our problems, concerns and dilemmas inside and out. He knows the up side, the down side, He knows them backward and forward and He knows the way out of them too. But we have to trust Him. He has time-proven methods and solutions, but we have to believe Him and obey Him. Solomon wrote:

Trust in the Lord with all thine heart; and lean not unto thine own understanding. In all thy ways acknowledge Him, and He shall direct thy paths (Proverbs 3:5-6).

One may say, "But God's way seems so illogical!" or "It's so contrary to what I feel like doing" or worse "If I do it God's way it will require faith!" (It seems we all have faith until we need it). But the blessed man will always trust in God's counsel before worldly counsel.

Truly serving God is a very serious matter. It's not a flippant, half-hearted decision to accept Him as your personal savior and then resort back to life as usual. It's true you can come to God just as you are, but you don't leave Him as you are. It's a decision to begin living according to His Word. That decision (when made sincerely) will change your life! Dietrich Bonhoeffer said, "When we are called to follow Christ, we are summoned to an exclusive attachment to His person.... The call goes forth and is at once followed by obedience...Christianity without obedience is always Christianity without Christ."

It seems a lot of people are "Christian" until it comes to obedience. But the true Christian embraces God's Word even when it's not comfortable or convenient. And Christianity is not always convenient. Just consider some of Jesus' "inconvenient" teachings. Let me encourage you to read them slowly and thoughtfully. Think how it would be to really live by them.

But I say unto you which hear, Love your enemies, do good to them which hate you, bless them that curse you, and pray for them which despitefully use you. And unto him that smiteth thee on the one cheek offer also the other; and him that taketh away thy cloke forbid not to take thy coat also. Give to every man that asketh of thee; and of him that taketh away thy goods ask them not again. And as ye would that men should do to you, do ye also to them likewise. For if ye love them which love you, what thank have ye? For sinners also love those that love them. And if ye do good to them which do good to you, what thank have ye? For sinners also do even the same. And if ye lend to them of whom ye hope to receive, what thank have ye? For sinners also lend to sinners, to receive as much again. But love ye your enemies, and do good, and lend, hoping for nothing again; and your reward shall be great and ye shall be the children of the Highest: for He is kind unto the unthankful and to the evil (Luke 6:27-35).

Wow! Still want to be a Christian? You see, true Christianity is very demanding. How about this one written by Peter:

For this is thankworthy, if a man for conscience toward God endure grief, suffering wrongfully. For what glory is it, if, when ye be buffeted for your faults ye shall take it patiently? but if, when ye do well, and suffer for it, ye take it patiently, this is acceptable with God. For even hereunto were ye called: because Christ also suffered for us, leaving us an example, that ye should follow his steps: who did no sin, neither was guile found in his mouth, who, when he was reviled, reviled not again; when he suffered he threatened not; but committed himself to him that judgeth righteously (I Peter 2:19-23).

Watch those aisle runners when this is preached! One of the major attributes of true Christianity is maintaining a good spirit and a polite attitude especially when things aren't going your way. When we are wronged for doing right remember God is the judge and He sees it all. Our attitude should be like Jesus' attitude who committed Himself to Him that judges righteously. The bottom line is that God is God. If we are willing to stick to His Word and do things His way, He will see us out one way or another. It may take several days or several years, but if we consistently endeavor to always do what's right, according to God's word He will judge righteously. A true test of Christianity is to take trials and offenses patiently for this is acceptable with God.

Many people's problems are prolonged, worsened or never solved at all because they don't do things God's way. Remember a true Christian obeys God's Word even when it's not comfortable. Are you still a Christian when the ugly realities of life occur or only when the church service is in high gear? I know it's heard much, but I don't think it's heeded much: unless you deny yourself you're not a disciple (Luke 9:23). Only when we decide to truly obey God's Word is the kingdom of God glorified. We could all very easily blend in and camouflage and be just like the rest of the world, but where would the glory be? Unless good works are seen the kingdom of God is not glorified.

Now I know these aren't the popular passages, but obedience to them truly sets one apart from those who merely profess Christianity. Paul said we should live no longer for ourselves but for Him who died for us (see II Corinthians 5:15). That really is asking a lot, isn't it? Remember there will always be many opinions thrown your way in the midst of your sufferings and dilemmas, but the blessed man will not walk in the counsel of the ungodly. He will obey God's Word even when it's inconvenient.

"... nor standeth in the way of sinners. . ."

CHAPTER TWO

One of the first things we must understand as children of God is the fact that we are called to walk a different course than the rest of the world. That fact seems to be a major stumbling block for a lot of would-be Christians. It is nevertheless a fundamental doctrine of authentic Christianity.

Perhaps you are familiar with the story of Israel's bondage in the nation of Egypt. The nation of Israel was God's chosen people, yet they were in slavery in a foreign land. So God raised up a leader by the name of Moses to be the man to lead them out. Now the king of Egypt wasn't too excited about God's plan and he refused to cooperate with Moses. So God began to pour out awful plagues on the nation of Egypt. He turned their water to blood. He sent an infestation of frogs. He caused an infestation of lice. He sent an infestation of flies. He caused all their cattle to die. He plagued their bodies with sores. He rained down hailstones and fire. He sent a plague of locusts to devour their crops. He covered the land with darkness for three days. Finally the firstborn of every man and beast suddenly died in one night (see Exodus 7-12). Guess what? The king finally conceded. A few days after Israel's mass exodus out of Egypt they found themselves at the shores of the Red Sea. Egypt's king had second thoughts and sent his military to wipe out the Israelites. With nowhere to turn suddenly God told Moses to extend his rod over the water, and when he did the sea divided before them. Israel walked safely across on dry land, but when the Egyptian army pursued them, the sea collapsed on them, and they were destroyed. Now here was the nation of Israel rejoicing safely on the other side of the sea. It was goodbye to Egypt! Goodbye to slavery! Goodbye to bondage! End of story, right? Wrong. Amongst this mass of humanity there were not many educated professionals. There were no scientists, doctors, princes or professors. There was only a mass of former slaves. But God was determined to transform this mass of slaves into a dignified, civilized and holy nation.

Ye have seen what I did unto the Egyptians, and how I bare you on eagles' wings, and brought you unto myself. Now therefore, if ye will obey my voice indeed, and keep my covenant, then ye shall be a peculiar treasure unto me above all people: for all the earth is mine: And ye shall be unto me a kingdom of priests, and an holy nation (Exodus 19:4-6).

One of the first things God did to dignify and separate them from the rest of humanity was give them a law. The law consisted of over six hundred commandments that governed them in matters of dress, diet, conduct and worship. This law is often referred to as the "Law of Moses." God desired them to be holy:

And the Lord spake unto Moses, saying, Speak unto all the congregation of the children of Israel, and say unto them, Ye shall be holy: for I the Lord your God am holy (Leviticus 19:1-2).

By their obedience to a unique way of life, with unique laws of holiness and ethics the whole world would become familiar with the one true God. They were to be examples in their lifestyle and behavior. God used them as a means to reveal Himself and His holiness to the rest of the world. In the New Testament era the church is given the same assignment!

As obedient children, not fashioning yourselves according to the former lusts in your ignorance, but as he which hath called you is holy, so be ye holy in all manner of conversation; because it is written, Be ye holy, for I am holy (I Peter 1:14-16).

That word translated "conversation" is αναστροφη (anastrophe) in Greek. It literally means behavior or conduct.

But ye are a chosen generation, a royal priesthood, an holy nation, a peculiar people; that ye should shew forth the praises of him who hath called you out of darkness into his marvelous light (I Peter 2:9).

The apostle Peter takes the same passages that were given to Israel and replants them firmly in the middle of New Testament theology. He gives them to the church. God's people are still called to be holy, pure, undefiled and separate from the rest of the world.

David said the blessed man doesn't stand in the way of sinners. What does it mean to stand in the way of sinners? Does it mean to stand in front of them and block their way? And if they try to go around you, you quickly step aside again to block them again? And if they turn around to leave you quickly run ahead of them and block the door? No. It means the blessed man isn't found walking or standing in the same path that the world walks. He doesn't blend in and conform to the course of this world.

Wherein in time past ye walked according to the course of this world...(Ephesians 2:2).

Not only does the blessed man reject the earthly and ungodly counsel and wisdom of this age (as seen in chapter 1) but he also refuses to acclimate and conform to its environment.

Enter ye in at the strait gate: for wide is the gate, and broad is the way, that leadeth to destruction, and many there be which go in thereat: because strait is the gate, and narrow is the way, which leadeth unto life, and few there be that find it (Matthew 7:13-14).

The world has a path that it walks and it leads to destruction. The children of God have a path too and it leads to eternal life.

Enter not into the path of the wicked, and go not in the way of evil men. Avoid it, pass not by it, turn from it, and pass away.... the path of the just is as the shining light, that shineth more and more unto the perfect day. The way of the wicked is as darkness: they know not at what they stumble (Proverbs 4:14, 15, 18, 19).

Now let me warn you, this path of righteousness runs contrary to the course of this world. You will be criticized. You will be mocked. You will be ridiculed.

When I was a little boy of about eight or nine years old, my father pastored a church in Atwater, California. Once a week we would have a children's service. We would play Bible games and sing songs but the one thing I especially looked forward to was when it was time to hear the story that our teacher was reading us. Her name was Sister Waddell and she was reading us a little book entitled *Pilgrim's Progress* by John Bunyan. It always seemed she would stop reading right at the most intriguing parts. I'd beg , "Please just read a little more!" And she'd smile and say, "You'll just have to come back next week." And oh, how I enjoyed hearing that story! It's a very well-known book in Christian literature; in fact, it's a classic. The story is about a little boy named Christian. Christian was on a journey to the celestial city. His instructions were simple: he was to follow this path all the way to the city. He was instructed and warned not to stray from the path. No matter what, he should never veer to the left or to the right. Well, Christian encountered many things to distract him. There was a giant and there was a place that he got so sleepy that he could hardly go a step further (I recommend this book not only for kids, but adults as well). The story is symbolic of our Christian walk. I always thought it would be fun to take a long journey on a path and experience some of the surprises and adventures that Christian experienced. But to literally walk this path of righteousness is not as simple and clean-cut as staying on a physical visible path. To literally walk this path of righteousness successfully we must consistently endeavor to do what's right in every situation that comes our way! That means the big things and the small things. How do we know what's right? We must align our decisions according to biblical principles and mandates. Let me emphasize again the big things and the small things. It's easy for us to believe God is concerned about the small things when it comes to our preferences and wishes. "Oh God, please get me a parking place close to the door!" "Oh Lord, please don't let my boss see me coming in late!" "Oh Lord, please let this check clear!" "Oh Lord, please help me find my keys!" If you were to ask, "Is it okay to pray about things like that?" you'd get something like, "Oh sure! God cares about even the little things. Why, even the very hairs of my head are numbered. He cares so much about even the little things in my life." But it seems that when it comes to His preferences and His wishes (like those pertaining to our appearance, apparel or adornment) you get, "Oh, He doesn't care about that. Those are small things!"

Paul said, "The things that I write unto you are the commandments of the Lord" (I Corinthians 14:37). No one has the authority to say those things don't matter. No one!

Peter said, "I will endeavor that ye may be able after my decease to have these things always in remembrance" (II Peter 1:15). In other words, even after Peter's dead and gone and his body is nothing more than bones and dust, his writings still apply. They matter.

Some ask why the apostles addressed issues that Jesus never mentioned. They wonder where they got their authority to do that. Notice a couple of things Jesus said. Keep in mind He's talking to His disciples:

But the comforter, which is the Holy Ghost, whom the Father will send in my name, he shall teach you all things, and bring all things to your remembrance, whatsoever I have said unto you (John 14:26).

Did you get that? They would be supernaturally empowered to remember everything He said to them. That's where they got their teachings! Jesus, still speaking to His disciples said:

I have yet many things to say unto you, but ye cannot bear them now. Howbeit when he, the Spirit of truth, is come, he will guide you into all truth (John 16:12-13).

When the apostles were finally filled with the Spirit in Acts 2 they were empowered to teach all truth. Nothing should have changed since. Our doctrine should not differ from that of the apostles. Seems to me we should all try to take the apostles' writings a little more seriously, even the "small" things. Remember we must consistently endeavor to do what's right in every situation that comes our way.

Proverbs 13:15 tells us "the way of a transgressor is hard." That's a cold, hard fact. This verse reveals the fact that there must be spiritual laws. And apparently if we attempt to violate these spiritual laws and disregard doing what is right, we will only prolong our suffering and frustrations. We don't break God's laws, we only break ourselves against His laws. Whatever a man sows, he reaps (Galatians 6:7). If you want to be a sower of discord (liar, trouble maker, gossiper), get ready for a lot of contention and strife. Remember, the truth is that most of the troubling situations people find themselves in are because of their own bad decisions. Sometimes we feel bad because we can't go back and re do certain things. But we can at least purpose to do right from this point on. In a word it's called repentance. Repentance is more than asking for forgiveness. It's purposing to do right from this point on. There's no situation that's too complex or difficult for God. But one must be willing to do things God's way. There's no alternative! When you're confused, perplexed and in darkness and you don't know which way to go, remember:

Thy word is a lamp unto my feet, and a light unto my path (Psalm 119:105).

So, if you're on the right path, stay on it. The blessed man won't walk in the path of sinners.

"... nor sitteth in the seat of the scornful..."

CHAPTER THREE

In I Kings 3 the Bible tells us that the Lord appeared to Solomon one night in a dream. Solomon had just succeeded the throne of his father David as the king of Israel. The Lord said to Solomon, "Ask what I shall give unto thee." Can you imagine God asking you that question? Solomon answered the Lord and said "Give therefore thy servant an understanding heart to judge thy people, that I may discern between good and bad." The Bible tells us that Solomon's request pleased God and the Lord said to Solomon: "Because you asked for wisdom rather than long life or wealth or rule over your enemies, behold I have given thee a wise and understanding heart, so that there was none like thee before thee, nor will there be another like thee." And the Lord went on to say, "And I have also given thee that which thou hast not asked, both riches, and honour: so that there shall not be any among the kings like unto thee all thy days." What a tremendous blessing! So Solomon became the wisest man that ever was. Solomon wrote three books of the Bible. He wrote the book of Proverbs, excluding the final two chapters. He wrote the book of Ecclesiastes and, of course, the Song of Solomon.

In the book of Ecclesiastes, he records some of his observations concerning the meaning of life. What is its goal and purpose?

I made me great works; I builded me houses; I planted me vineyards: I made me gardens and orchards, and I planted trees in them of all kinds of fruits: I made me pools of water, to water therewith the wood that bringeth forth trees: I got me servants and maidens, and had servants born in my house; also I had great possessions of great and small cattle above all that were in Jerusalem before me: I gathered me also silver and gold, and the peculiar treasure of kings and of the provinces: I gat me men singers and women singers, and the delights of the sons of men, as musical instruments, and that of all sorts. So I was great, and increased more than all that were before me in Jerusalem: also my wisdom remained with me. And whatsoever mine eyes desired I kept not from them, I withheld not my heart from any joy; for my heart rejoiced in all my labour: and this was my portion of all my labour (Ecclesiastes 2:4-10).

It would appear from all external observations that Solomon's life was perfect and he was the happiest man in the world. But notice the next verse:

Then I looked on all the works that my hands had wrought, and on the labour that I had laboured to do: And, behold, all was vanity and vexation of spirit, and there was no profit under the sun (Ecclesiastes 2:11).

28

This word "vanity" means unprofitable, meaningless or unfulfilling. This word "vexation" means saddening or grief causing. A consistent theme throughout the book of Ecclesiastes is a reminder that without God life is vanity. Finally at the conclusion of the book of Ecclesiastes is found what I believe to be perhaps the most profound and significant statement ever declared. Solomon wrote:

Let us hear the conclusion of the whole matter: Fear God, and keep his commandments: for this is the whole duty of man (Ecclesiastes 12:13).

Now this passage is not relegated only to Old Covenant theology or doctrine. This commandment still applies today, even in the twenty-first-century New Testament church. We will observe that shortly.

David said the blessed man doesn't sit in the seat of the scornful. That means he doesn't occupy the place of the scornful, nor does he sit where scorners talk. He's not one with them. Well, what does it mean to be scornful? To be scornful means to be full of mockery or ridicule. In a biblical context it refers to those who make light of godly things. Scornful people belittle and scoff at things that are holy and righteous.

Several years ago I heard the story about an event that happened to a well-respected district official in the United Pentecostal Church. This official was presiding over a meeting in a church that had been having some problems. As he began to address some of the causes of the problems a disgruntled man got out of his seat and stood in the aisle and began to mockingly bow over and over before the official like a slave before his master. "Is this what you want?" the man said. Then he began to crawl on the floor in a sarcastic display of mock humility. The official made it clear that was not what he wanted. Very shortly following the meeting the man was violently robbed and beaten by a gang of street thugs. He was beaten so badly that his mind was never quite the same as it was before. This event calls to mind the scripture that says, "Judgments are prepared for scorners and stripes for the back of fools" (Proverbs 19:29).

Psalm 111:10 says that the fear of the Lord is the beginning of wisdom. When a person has a sobering reverence toward God and an awareness of His judgments and wrath, that person is not a confused idiot, but he is standing on the foundation of a healthy relationship with God. He is in the prime position to begin learning about God. It is the beginning of wisdom.

Notice what Solomon wrote about the scorners that reject wisdom:

Wisdom crieth without; she uttereth her voice in the streets: She crieth in the chief place of concourse, in the openings of the gates: in the city she uttereth her words, saying, How long, ye simple ones, will ye love simplicity? and the scorners delight in their scorning, and fools hate knowledge? Turn you at my reproof: behold, I will pour out my spirit unto you, I will make known my words unto you. Because I have called, and ye refused; I have stretched out my hand, and no man regarded...for that they hated knowledge, and did not choose the fear of the Lord (Proverbs 1:20-24,29).

This is the pivotal point, the distinguishing factor between the blessed man and the scorners: The blessed man fears God. The scorners do not fear God. The fear of the Lord is what separates the blessed man from the scornful.

Now I know this may cross a lot of popular theology, but; to fear God is a very beautiful and precious thing. It can save you a lot of heartache and misery. Some say, "Well, that's Old Testament mentality and Old Testament theology to fear God!" Maybe someone should have informed Jesus and the apostles of that, because they said things like:

fear God... (I Peter 2:17).

And I say unto you my friends, Be not afraid of them that kill the body, and after that have no more that they can do. But I will forewarn you whom ye shall fear: Fear him, which after he hath killed hath power to cast into hell; yea, I say unto you, Fear him (Luke 12:4-5).

His mercy is on them that fear him from generation to generation (Luke 1:50).

But in every nation he that feareth him, and worketh righteousness, is accepted with him (Acts 10:35).

Whosoever among you feareth God, to you is the word of this salvation sent (Acts 13:26).

Well; because of unbelief they were broken off, and thou standest by faith. Be not high-minded, but fear: for if God spared not the natural branches, take heed lest he also spare not thee. Behold therefore the goodness and severity of God: on them which fell, severity; but toward thee, goodness, if thou continue in his goodness: otherwise thou also shalt be cut off (Romans 11:20-22).

Let us cleanse ourselves from all filthiness of the flesh and spirit, perfecting holiness in the fear of God (II Corinthians 7:1).

Submitting yourselves one to another in the fear of God (Ephesians 5:21).

The fear of the Lord is a precious thing. It is the factor that will separate you from the scorners and mockers. I know we're not supposed to admit this, but sometimes it's fear of God that motivates us and prompts us to do what's right. There is nothing wrong with that. I know I'm crossing a lot of popular theology, but I'm just saying what the Bible says.

It's possible to love God with all of your heart and to be experiencing His grace and yet fear Him at the same time. Genesis 6:8 tells us "Noah found grace in the eyes of the Lord," yet:

By faith Noah, being warned of God of things not seen as yet, moved with fear, prepared an ark...(Hebrews 11:7).

Even godly, righteous, grace-experiencing Noah feared God and obeyed Him.

Proverbs 19:29 tells us, "Judgments are prepared for scorners, and stripes for the back of fools." The scorners abound in their foolishness and sufferings because they "did not choose the fear of the Lord" (Proverbs 1:29). But since the blessed man fears God, he will not be found sitting in the seat of the scornful.

"But his delight is in the law of the Lord; and in his law doth he meditate day and night."

CHAPTER FOUR

History tells us that in A.D. 312 there was an emperor of Rome named Constantine. This was a time when Christianity was under strong persecution. We are told that before the battle of Milvian Bridge Constantine prayed for help in obtaining the victory in this battle. Following his prayer a cross appeared in the sky with the words "In this sign conquer." Following this incident Constantine converted to Christianity. All of a sudden it became popular to be a "Christian." Constantine gave Christianity somewhat of a celebrity status. He protected the church. He built church buildings with Roman revenue. He exempted the ministry from taxes (imagine how many felt the call). Naturally, at this time much paganism began to creep into Christianity. There evolved an intermingling between the church and the world. Christianity was now trendy. The result of this, of course, was a lot of insincerity within the faith.

In a similar sense I believe we live in the same kind of environment today. Not in that Christianity is necessarily popular or trendy, but in the sense that there are many who claim to be "Christian" but do not live by the teachings of true biblical Christianity. They lack the willingness and sincerity to adhere seriously to all that Jesus and the apostles taught.

David said the blessed man delights in the law of the Lord and meditates in it day and night. Here's a tidbit of information: The majority of the world does not delight in the law of the Lord. But just because truth is unpopular doesn't mean that truth is unimportant. Here's another tidbit of information: The original apostolic doctrine of the New Testament church is not popular either. Sadly, the original doctrine of the apostles isn't popular among a lot of so-called Christians today. It's a sad day when normal New Testament Christianity becomes abnormal. Modern Christianity eagerly accepts and proclaims the teachings of grace, but at the same time ignores many other plain and obvious commandments of Scripture. Now whether we like to admit it or not, God has rules. I know that's a hard fact for some to accept, but it's true. Otherwise Jesus wouldn't have said:

Ye are my friends, if ye do whatsoever I command you (John 15:14).

He that hath my commandments, and keepeth them, he it is that loveth me... (John 14:21).

Not only does God have rules, but obedience to these rules is very important:

Not every one that saith unto me, Lord, Lord, shall enter into the kingdom of heaven; but he that doeth the will of my Father which is in heaven. Many will say to me in that day, Lord, Lord, have we not prophesied in thy name? and in thy name have cast out devils? and in thy name done many wonderful works? And then will I profess unto them, I never knew you: depart from me, ye that work iniquity (Matthew 7:21-23).

And why call ye me, Lord, Lord, and do not the things which I say? (Luke 6:46).

Jesus told His disciples to go into all nations and teach them "to observe all things whatsoever I have commanded you" (Matthew 28:20).

In I Corinthians 14:37 Paul said, "The things that I write unto you are the commandments of the Lord." Apparently God has rules even for the New Testament church of the twenty-first century.

The blessed man delights in the law of the Lord day and night. This word "delight" means to find pleasing, to hold in high value or esteem. The reason why God's law is so precious to the blessed man is that he understands how it can save him from a lot of heartache and trouble. Those that sincerely fear God and serve God are spared a lot of the troubles that common humanity has to deal with. For example, those that truly serve God know and understand that sexual relations are intended to be between one man and one woman in the context of marriage only. Therefore they are not concerned about contracting sexually transmitted diseases like the world is.

Wherewithal shall a young man cleanse his way? By taking heed thereto according to thy word (Psalm 119:9).

If a boy or a girl decides to serve God at a very young age, he or she will be spared many of the binding habits and addictions that others might have to contend with. Why? Because of obedience to His word.

Unless thy law had been my delights, I should then have perished in mine affliction (Psalm 119:92).

I will walk at liberty: for I seek thy precepts (Psalm 119:45).

God's laws aren't designed to hinder us or burden us; they are designed to spare us a lot of heartache and suffering. The blessed man delights in the law of the Lord day and night. He doesn't painstakingly examine God's Word searching for loopholes and escape clauses to find how he can get by without obeying God's Word. No, he enthusiastically examines and searches for what pleases God! He ponders and considers His Word day and night. He applies it to his daily living and decision making. He willingly allows it to govern his life. He has a childlike faith toward the scriptures. There's no debating and twisting of meaning. It means what it says and says what it means. He delights in the law of the Lord!

I do not know of anyone in the Bible that had a passion for God like David did. I know there were many that loved God and served Him. They were faithful and dedicated to the end. But I can't think of anyone that had a passion for God like David did. He was a man after God's own heart (Acts 13:22). Recently I was considering some of the other psalms that David wrote and how his passion is so evident and brilliantly expressed in them.

As the hart panteth after the waterbrooks, so

panteth my soul after thee, O God (Psalm 42:1).

The hart was a small deer. Picture in your mind the hart desperately running through the wilderness. He is pursued by a hunter, his breathing is heavy, and his mouth is dry. The day is warm and sunny, and, he needs a drink of cold refreshing water, but he knows it's dangerous to stop. Sooner or later he has to make it to the cool brook to quench his raging thirst. That describes the passion that David possessed for God.

I opened my mouth, and panted: for I longed for thy commandments (Psalm 119:131).

Such an intense and genuine desire for God's ways! I mean think about it, writing poetry about God and His Word! David was nothing less than obsessed with God! You cannot have a passion for God without having a passion for His Word at the same time.

Psalm 119 is the longest chapter in the entire Bible. There are 176 verses. Only six verses do not mention His ordinances, His word, His judgments, His commandments, His statutes, His precepts, His testimonies or His law. One cannot write like that with a feigned love. That is a passion for God's Word!

The Bible expresses the very mind, character and will of God. Besides the person of Jesus Christ it is the most precise, specific and detailed expression of who God is. In His Word are expressed His preferences, His likes, His dislikes and His expectations. If you love Him you'll love His Word too. David said the blessed man delights in the law of the Lord and he meditates in it day and night. That's the fourth habit of the blessed man. May God grant us such a passion for His Word!

"And he shall be like a tree planted by the rivers of water, that bringeth forth his fruit in his season; his leaf also shall not wither; and whatsoever he doeth shall prosper."

CHAPTER FIVE

Up to this point we have observed the four characteristics or habits of the blessed man. Next we are going to observe the benefits of living by these characteristics. Now before we go any further it is very important that I emphasize the fact that these four characteristics are profoundly life-altering characteristics~not only in the sense of the blessings that you will experience, but in the sense of the serious decision you are making in choosing to live by them. Please do not consider this book to be merely a quick, easy, four-step plan of how to get blessed by God. Each of these four characteristics are major paradigms. They will cause you to radically change your life (if you sincerely choose to live by them). They will revolutionize your lifestyle. If you choose to adopt these characteristics you will begin to think and behave in ways that starkly contrast with those of popular North American culture. It is not a small decision. Occasionally you will even have to think and behave in ways that diametrically oppose your own self-will and personal preferences. That is an element of true Christianity. These four characteristics will compel you to embrace ideas, philosophies and habits that others will consider meaningless and absurd. So before we go any further, take a moment to look at them again and seriously ponder their significance. They are found in the first two verses of Psalm 1.

We all decide for ourselves the level of commitment or the degree to which we will live by the Word of God. God does not force us to obey His Word. He simply states what is expected and then leaves the decision to us. The Bible is also a very practical book. It is not usually overly descriptive nor does it always explain why certain things are written or demanded by God. When you consider the fact that Jesus spent three and one-half years ministering and training his disciples, yet the teachings that are recorded in the Bible could be read literally in a few days, you realize that obviously whatever is written is very important. We cannot pick and choose which scriptures matter and which ones don't. John said:

And there are also many other things which Jesus did, the which, if they should be written every one, I suppose that even the world itself could not contain the books that should be written. Amen (John 21:25).

Apparently, what we have contained in our little hand-held Bibles is of utmost importance.

Perhaps one of the most exhausting and frustrating things to have to contend with is a sick baby. Ask any mother. When a baby is sick it is very rare for the child to willingly, cooperatively take his medicine. He kicks. He squirms. He cries. He wrestles. He turns his head. He pushes it away. The medicine spills. It gets everywhere

44

except where it needs to be. Babies usually refuse to simply open their mouths and receive what will heal them and cause them to feel better. The reason that they fight and contend with you is because they don't understand the benefit. All they know is that they don't want it in their face and they really wish you would quit trying to stick it in their mouth. They're not in the mood for this foolishness right now! They don't understand the benefit. Since you can't communicate to them the purpose and the function of the medicine, the battle wages on. Therefore they may suffer longer, harboring the sickness within them. But when we mature and understand the purpose of the medicine, we willingly take it all by ourselves~even if it tastes bad. In fact, we'll mark the time and watch the clock to make sure we take the next dosage at the required time. Pretty soon we're feeling better and we're back in our routine like nothing ever happened.

This illustrates two types of Christians. The immature Christian and the mature Christian. The immature Christians aren't interested in the deeper things of God and His Word. They don't care about doctrine. They don't care about truth. They don't care about holiness or separation from the world. They don't care about giving. They don't care about their attitude or obedience. All they know is they got saved and they believe in Jesus and that's all they really care about now. To them all that other stuff is yucky! It tastes bad! So they squirm and resist and turn their heads, never experiencing the deeper dimensions and blessings of truly worshipping God. The writer of Hebrews said:

For when for the time ye ought to be teachers, ye have need that one teach you again which be the first

45

principles of the oracles of God; and are become such as have need of milk, and not of strong meat. For every one that useth milk is unskillful in the word of righteousness: for he is a babe. But strong meat belongeth to them that are of full age, even those who by reason of use have their senses exercised to discern both good and evil. Therefore leaving the principles of the doctrine of Christ, let us go on unto perfection; not laying again the foundation of repentance from dead works, and of faith toward God, of the doctrine of baptisms, and of laying on of hands, and of resurrection of the dead, and of eternal judgment (Hebrews 5:12-6:2).

According to the writer of Hebrews, repentance is a foundation. Spirit baptism is a foundation. Water baptism is a foundation. However, we should all eventually come to a point where we move on from there and learn more about the Word of God. To such a degree that we can teach others. The term "leaving the principles of the doctrine of Christ" does not mean abandoning them, but going on from there.

The spiritually healthy Christian eventually begins to crave a knowledge concerning the deeper things of God. The mature Christian willingly swallows the healing remedy of the Word of God. It's like a medicine to his soul. So he grows and he prospers and he enters the realm of the blessed man and reaps the spiritual blessings thereof.

The blessed man is likened to a tree planted by the rivers of water. It's not a wild tree that just happened to sprout one day; it's a planted tree. It is purposely and intentionally placed and established by God. It is not just planted anywhere either. It is carefully planted right next

46

to the source of its life, a flowing river. First of all the blessed man is spiritually stable. As the tree's roots are deeply and firmly entrenched into the nourishing soil, so is the blessed man firmly established by his faith in God. The blessed man is stedfast and unmoveable. Because of his confidence in God he truly understands the fact that life's storms and trials are temporary. He is not devastated and uprooted by the winds of opposition that occasionally rage against him. His faith is firmly rooted in God.

We are warned in the Word of God to expect opposition and trials of faith. They're normal. Notice what Jesus said to Peter:

And the Lord said, Simon, Simon, behold, Satan hath desired to have you, that he may sift you as wheat: But I have prayed for thee, that thy faith fail not: and when thou art converted, strengthen thy brethren (Luke 22:31-32).

Jesus didn't pray that Peter would be spared from all opposition and trials. He didn't pray that Peter would have peace, health and wealth all the days of his life. He prayed that his faith wouldn't fail! Peter came to know about suffering and persecution but his faith never failed. In fact Peter was able to minister and encourage others in their sufferings:

Beloved, think it not strange concerning the fiery trial which is to try you, as though some strange thing happened unto you: But rejoice, inasmuch as ye are partakers of Christ's sufferings; that when his glory shall be revealed, ye may be glad also with exceeding joy. If ye be reproached for the name of Christ, happy are ye; for the Spirit of glory and of God resteth upon you:

on their part he is evil spoken of, but on your part he is glorified...yet if any man suffer as a Christian, let him not be ashamed; but let him glorify God on this behalf (I Peter 4:12-14,16).

Paul warned also:

Yea, and all that will live godly in Christ Jesus shall suffer persecution (II Timothy 3:12).

Through it all we must maintain absolute faith and trust in God. Even when it seems like He's nowhere around. Some lose their faith in God in the midst of physical afflictions. When one is plagued with a sickness it doesn't mean that God has forsaken them. It doesn't mean that God is unable to heal them. It doesn't mean that they are faithless. It means they now have to use another kind of faith. Not the kind that is "positive thinking" but the kind that trusts God no matter what. Physical affliction is not an indicator of the absence of God. Paul told Timothy, "Use a little wine for thy stomach's sake, and thine often infirmities" (I Timothy 5:23). Apparently, Timothy was sick a lot. Does this mean God was unable to heal him? Does it mean Paul or Timothy or the church did not have faith? No, it simply meant he would have to trust God in spite of his affliction. Paul also wrote:

Trophimus have I left at Miletum sick (II Timothy 4:20).

Trophimus was a fellow laborer with Paul. It's very likely they prayed for healing, but he remained sick. Does this mean something's wrong? God's not a healer after all? No, it means sometimes He does heal and sometimes He doesn't. Our responsibility is to trust Him *either* way. Read Hebrews 11 sometime. You'll notice the first part deals with those that accomplished great exploits through faith.Then at verse 36 the tone changes. Others were afflicted and tormented, yet all of them had faith (Hebrews 11:39). Some's faith delivered them from trials while others' faith sustained them through trials. Through it all we must maintain faith and trust in God. Faith is not an emotion. It's a conscious, intelligent decision to wholeheartedly believe God regardless of external circumstances or internal emotions. The blessed man is like a tree planted by the rivers of water. He is sustained, strengthened, and nourished by God every moment of his life!

Not only is it an intentionally planted tree flourishing by the river, but it's a fruit-bearing tree as well. A healthy, fruit- producing tree is designed to benefit others. I've never heard of a fruit-eating tree. The blessed man is divinely empowered to edify, encourage, enlighten and even educate those around him. Because of the decisions he made a long time ago he begins to emerge as a source of blessings to those around him. His godly attributes are witnessed and observed by his family and peers. He maintains a calm and polite attitude in the midst of misunderstanding, disagreements and even false accusations. Remember, after all, he trusts God in every situation. It's not just a verbal profession. He really believes God is in control.

Look at what Jesus taught:

I am the true vine, and my father is the husbandman. Every branch in me that beareth not fruit he taketh away: and every branch that beareth fruit, he purgeth it, that it may bring forth more fruit. Now ye are clean through the word which I have spoken unto you. Abide in me, and I in you. As the branch cannot bear fruit of itself, except it abide in the vine; No more can ye, except ye abide in me. I am the vine, ye are the branches: He that abideth in me, and I in him, the same bringeth forth much fruit: For without me ye can do nothing (John 15:1-5).

Jesus commands us to bear fruit, yet He makes it plain we can bear no fruit without Him. What is the fruit that He produces?

But the fruit of the Spirit is love, joy, peace, longsuffering, gentleness, goodness, faith, meekness, temperance: against such there is no law (Galatians 5:22-23).

The godly attributes that proceed from within us are an act of the Spirit of God.

Trees are very vulnerable and defenseless. When a forest fire sweeps across the land the trees don't pull up roots and start running for safety. They have to remain and endure the threatening environment. Even the blessed man may occasionally find his environment harsh and threatening. But because he's tapped into the living waters, the elements and conditions around him don't alter or faze him. He maintains godliness regardless of his environment. David said, "His leaf also shall not wither." As long as the roots are tapped in to the water supply, the tree thrives. Even the smallest leaves remain supple and healthy.

David added, "And whatsoever he doeth shall prosper." Remember this is the individual abiding in God, and God in him (John 15:1-5). He's separate from the world, living in godliness, obedient to the Scripture. Our definition of prosperity and God's definition of prosperity are two different things. Our idea is money, wealth and material possessions. God's idea of prosperity is an individual allowing God to direct his life. From God's perspective, that's when an individual is prospering.

And unto the angel of the church in Smyrna write; these things saith the first and the last, which was dead, and is alive; I know thy works, and tribulation, and poverty, (but thou art rich)...(Rev. 2:8-9).

To the persecuted church in Smyrna God was saying, "On the outside you're poor and lacking and poverty- stricken, but in my eyes you're rich!" Notice that God considered them rich because of their works and their faithfulness in tribulation. These are the things that matter to God. If a person is plentiful in faith and good works, then that person is prosperous! He is a healthy, fruit-bearing tree planted by the waters.

"The ungodly are not so, but are like the chaff which the wind driveth away."

54

CHAPTER SIX

As we have seen in the previous chapter, the godly man is truly blessed. He is like a tree planted by the river of living waters. But according to Psalm 1:5 the ungodly are not so. In contrast to a healthy, fruit-bearing tree the ungodly are likened to nothing more than chaff. It is not that they are invaluable as individual human beings, but that a life lived without serving God ultimately is a life of vanity:

For what shall it profit a man, if he shall gain the whole world, and lose his own soul? (Mark 8:36).

Chaff is the thin, empty shell of a grain stem. It is very light and easily taken by the wind after harvesting. There are other passages of Scripture that describe the ungodly as chaff:

Let them be confounded and put to shame that seek after my soul: let them be turned back and brought to confusion that devise my hurt. Let them be as chaff before the wind: and let the angel of the Lord chase them (Psalm 35:4-5).

Therefore as the fire devoureth the stubble, and the flame consumeth the chaff, so their root shall be as rottenness, and their blossom shall go up as dust: because they have cast away the law of the Lord of hosts, and despised the word of the Holy One of Israel (Isaiah 5:24).

Moreover the multitude of thy strangers shall be like small dust, and the multitude of the terrible ones shall be as chaff that passeth away: yea, it shall be at an instant suddenly (Isaiah 29:5).

Chaff is used as an analogy to describe the emptiness and vanity of a life without God.

So according to the first psalm the godly man is blessed. The ungodly are not blessed. Sometimes ungodly and rebellious people may seem blessed, but in reality they are not blessed at all. Notice what Job observed concerning the wealth of the wicked:

Wherefore do the wicked live, become old, yea, are mighty in power? Their seed is established in their sight with them, and their offspring before their eyes. Their houses are safe from fear, neither is the rod of God upon them. Their bull gendereth, and faileth not; their cow calveth, and casteth not her calf. They send forth their little ones like a flock, and their children dance. They take the timbrel and harp, and rejoice at the sound of the organ. They spend their days in wealth, and in a moment go down to the grave. Therefore they say unto God, depart from us; for we desire not the knowledge of thy ways. What is the Almighty, that we should serve him? and what profit should we have, if we pray unto

Him? Lo, their good is not in their hand: the counsel of the wicked is far from me. How oft is the candle of the wicked put out! And how oft cometh their destruction upon them! God distributeth sorrows in his anger. They are as stubble before the wind, and as chaff that the storm carrieth away (Job 21:7-18).

Possessions, education, social status, positions, titles or money matter nothing if one's soul is lost. Material possessions and money are not signs of acceptance or approval with God. There's another kind of wealth that is much more valuable than money. It's possessing a knowledge of God and choosing to serve Him above all else. This is known as being "rich toward God":

"...The ground of a certain rich man brought forth plentifully: And he thought within himself, saying, What shall I do, because I have no room where to bestow my fruits? And he said, This will I do: I will pull down my barns, and build greater; and there will I bestow all my fruits and my goods. And I will say to my soul, Soul, thou hast much goods laid up for many years; take thine ease, eat, drink, and be merry. But God said unto him, Thou fool, this night thy soul shall be required of thee: then whose shall those things be, which thou hast provided? So is he that layeth up treasure for himself, and is not rich toward God (Luke 12:16-21).

I believe that we all occasionally fall prey to that kind of thinking~the kind of thinking that ignores the eternal and emphasizes the temporary. Psalm 73 was written by a man named Asaph.This man nearly lost his faith when he pondered the prosperity of the wicked. For your convenience the entire passage is included here:

Truly God is good to Israel, even to such as are of a clean heart. But as for me, my feet were almost gone; my steps had well nigh slipped. For I was envious at the foolish, when I saw the prosperity of the wicked. For there are no bands in their death: but their strength is firm. They are not in trouble as other men; neither are they plagued like other men. Therefore pride compasseth them about as a chain; violence covereth them as a garment. Their eyes stand out with fatness: they have more than heart could wish. They are corrupt, and speak wickedly concerning oppression: they speak loftily. They set their mouth against the heavens, and their tongue walketh through the earth. Therefore his people return hither: and waters of a full cup are wrung out to them. And they say, how doth God know? and is there knowledge in the most High? Behold, these are the ungodly, who prosper in the world; they increase in riches. Verily I have cleansed my heart in vain, and washed my hands in innocency. For all the day long have I been plagued, and chastened every morning. If I say, I will speak thus; behold, I should offend against the generation of thy children. When I thought to know this, it was too painful for me; Until I went into the sanctuary of God; then understood I their end. Surely thou didst set them in slippery places: thou castedst them down into destruction. How are they brought into desolation, as in a moment! They are utterly consumed with terrors. As a dream when one awaketh; so, O Lord, when thou awakest, thou shalt despise their image. Thus my heart was grieved, and I was pricked in my reins. So foolish was I, and ignorant: I was as a beast before thee. Nevertheless I am continually with thee: thou hast holden me by my right hand. Thou shalt guide me with thy counsel, and afterward receive me to glory. Whom have I in heaven but thee? and there is none upon earth that I desire beside thee. My flesh and my heart faileth: but God is the strength of my heart, and my portion forever. For, lo, they that are far from thee shall perish: thou hast destroyed all them that go a whoring from thee. But it is good for me to draw near to God: I have put my trust in the Lord God, that I may declare all thy works (Psalm 73).

I think we can relate to Asaph, can't we? Sometimes it seems we endeavor to do right and live right all to no avail. Meanwhile the God-haters and the rebels of our culture live in mansions and ride in limousines. They don't worry about paying bills. They don't worry about leaking roofs, smog test failures or broken transmissions. Money solves all their problems. This is the attitude that Asaph had until he went to the sanctuary of God. It was just too much to bear so he decided to go to "church." And it was there he pondered and meditated and came to his senses. He considered their end. He realized his portion and his eternal reward. Going to church can work wonders for you. It is there that we pull back the veil of vanity and focus on what really matters. I've heard it said, "I'm closer to God on a fishing trip than I ever am sitting on a pew. When I see the beautiful mountains and trees and feel the warm sunshine, that's all I need." These are the sentiments of those that in reality are too lazy, undisciplined, or just too uninterested in God to come to church. God gave the beauty of creation to let us know there is a God, to prove His existence. But he gave pastors, apostles, prophets, evangelists and teachers for the perfecting of the saints

(Ephesians 4:11). There's no tree or mountain or river that's going to pray for your children, teach you a Bible study or tell you how to be saved. The ministry is from God. Since our fleshly nature is so easily persuaded to overly indulge in material matters, a discipline needs to be developed to keep our minds on eternal issues. Regular worship and faithful church attendance help us to align our priorities (see Hebrews 10:25). When Asaph took the time to worship God he no longer had the victim mentality. Regardless of the wealth of others, he was satisfied enough to declare, "Whom have I in heaven but thee?" A knowledge of the one true God is worth more than anything! David declared:

Fret not thyself because of evildoers, neither be thou envious against the workers of iniquity.... for evildoers shall be cut off: but those that wait upon the Lord, they shall inherit the earth (Psalm 37:1,9).

When all is said and done, the godly man is truly blessed, while the ungodly are not.

"Therefore the ungodly shall not stand in the judgment, nor sinners in the congregation of the righteous. For the Lord knoweth the way of the righteous, but the way of the ungodly shall perish."

CHAPTER SEVEN

The Incarnation (God's manifestation of Himself in flesh) was perhaps the greatest event in the history of mankind. It is commonly understood that the manifestation of God in the person of Jesus Christ was a necessary event in order to ultimately grant us access to God. But did you know that the Incarnation also justly qualifies God to judge us? The following story points that out:

Billions of people were scattered on a great plain before God's throne. Some of the groups near the front talked heatedly~not with cringing shame, but with belligerence. "How can God judge us?" said one. "What does He know about suffering?" snapped a woman. She jerked back a sleeve to reveal a tattooed number from a Nazi concentration camp. "We endured terror, beatings, torture, death!" In another group a black man lowered his collar. "What about this?" he demanded, showing an ugly rope burn, "lynched for no crime but being black! We have suffocated in slave ships, been torn from *loved ones, and toiled till death gave release." Far out across the plain were hundreds of such groups. Each had a complaint against God for the evil and suffering He permitted in His world. How lucky God was to live in heaven where there was no weeping, no fear, no hunger, no hatred! Indeed, what did God know about what man had been forced to endure in this world? "After all, God leads a pretty sheltered life," they said.*

So each group sent out a leader, chosen because he had suffered the most. There was a Jew, a black, an untouchable from India, an illegitimate, a person from Hiroshima and one from a Siberian slave camp. In the center of the plain they consulted with each other. At last they were ready to present their case. It was rather simple: before God would be qualified to be their judge, He must endure what they had endured. Their decision was that God should be sentenced to live on earth~as a man!

But because He was God, they set certain safeguards to be sure He could not use His divine powers to help Himself: Let Him be born a Jew. Let the legitimacy of His birth be doubted, so that none would know who is really His father. Let Him champion a cause so just but so radical that it brings down upon Him the hate, the condemnation, and efforts of every major traditional and established religious authority to eliminate Him. Let Him try to describe what no man has ever seen, tasted, heard or smelled. Let Him try to communicate God to men. Let Him be betrayed by His dearest friends. Let Him be indicted on false charges, tried before a prejudiced jury, and convicted by a cowardly judge. Let Him see what it is to be terribly alone and completely abandoned by every living thing. Let Him be tortured and let Him die! Let Him die the most humiliating death~with common thieves.

As each leader announced his portion of the sentence, loud murmurs of approval went up from the great throngs of people. But when the last had finished pronouncing sentence, there was a long silence. No one uttered another word. No one moved. For suddenly all knew...God had already served His sentence. 1

God is more than a detached observer in the sky. Because He took upon Himself full and complete humanity in the person of Jesus Christ, and experienced all of the weakness, frailty and temptations of humanity, he is qualified to be our judge.

God is also a just God. He is a God of justice. He is not an unbiased observer but He is actively concerned and aware of the affairs and activities of humanity. He does reward and He does punish according to people's deeds and activities. Notice what Solomon wrote:

Many seek the ruler's favour; but every man's judgment cometh from the Lord (Proverbs 29:26).

This reminds me of a little saying I have that says "If you displease God it doesn't matter who you please, but if you please God it doesn't matter who you displease." Consider these passages as well:

...God shall judge the righteous and the wicked: for there is a time there for every purpose and for every work (Ecclesiastes 3:17).

But we are sure that the judgment of God is according to truth against them which commit such things. And thinkest thou this, O man, that judgest them which do such things, and doest the same, that thou shalt escape the judgment of God? Or despisest thou the riches of his goodness and forbearance and longsuffering; not knowing that the goodness of God leadeth thee to repentance? But after thy hardness and impenitent heart treasurest up unto thyself wrath against the day of wrath and revelation of the righteous judgment of God; who will render to every man according to his deeds: To them who by patient continuance in well doing seek for glory and honour and immortality, eternal life: But unto them that are contentious, and do not obey the truth, but obey unrighteousness, indignation and wrath, Tribulation and anguish, upon every soul of man that doeth evil, of the Jew first, and also of the Gentile; But glory, honour, and peace, to every man that worketh good, to the Jew first, and also to the Gentile: For there is no respect of persons with God (Romans 2:2-11).

Knowing that of the Lord ye shall receive the reward of the inheritance: for ye serve the Lord Christ. But he that doeth wrong shall receive for the wrong which he hath done: and there is no respect of persons (Colossians 3:24-25).

Seeing it is a righteous thing with God to recompense tribulation to them that trouble you; And to you who are troubled rest with us, when the Lord Jesus shall be revealed from heaven with his mighty angels, In flaming fire taking vengeance on them that know not God, and that obey not the gospel of our Lord Jesus Christ; Who shall be punished with everlasting destruction from the presence of the Lord, and from the glory of his power (II Thessalonians 1:6-9).

These are some very sobering passages that remind us of the justice of God and the importance of living right before Him (see also Galatians 6:7-8; II Peter 3:7-11 and Revelation 20:11-13). Keep in mind the Christian is spared the wrath of God provided that he maintains absolute faith in Jesus Christ. That is, he believes Jesus is who He says He is and that His word is pure truth, and he endeavors to obey it. Thankfully we are granted the promise of I John 1:9: "If we confess our sins he is faithful and just to forgive us our sins, and to cleanse us from all unrighteousness." And Hebrews 4:16, "Let us therefore come boldly unto the throne of grace, that we may obtain mercy, and find grace to help in time of need." It is those that reject Jesus and His plan of salvation that have no defense against the wrath of God. That is what is meant when David said that the ungodly shall not "stand" in the judgment. John put it this way:

For the great day of his wrath is come; and who shall be able to stand? (Revelation 6:17).

David also added that sinners would not be numbered with the congregation of the righteous. In David's day God's "congregation" was the nation of Israel. They were God's chosen people with whom He had a covenant. Acts 15:14 tells us that God is now visiting the Gentiles to take out of them a people for His name. That's the church! The Greek word translated "church" is εκκλησια (ekklesia). It literally means "called out" or "separate." The church is now God's "congregation" of the righteous.

To be in God's church there are certain stipulations. First, we must have absolute faith in Jesus Christ. Genuine faith in Jesus compels us to heed His teachings concerning salvation. Jesus taught repentance:

I came not to call the righteous, but sinners to repentance (Luke 5:32).

"...except ye repent, ye shall all likewise perish (Luke 13:3).

Remember that repentance is more than asking for forgiveness; it's making a change to purpose to live according to God's Word. Jesus also taught the importance of baptism:

He that believeth and is baptized shall be saved...(Mark 16:16).

Jesus also taught that those who believe in Him should be filled with the Holy Ghost:

He that believeth on me, as the scripture hath said, out of his belly shall flow rivers of living water. (But this spake he of the Spirit, which they that believe on him should receive: for the Holy Ghost was not yet given; because that Jesus was not yet glorified (John 7:38-39).

The apostles of Jesus were divinely empowered by the Spirit of God to teach all truth. They further endorsed these same primary factors. The apostles taught repentance:

And the times of this ignorance God winked at; but now commandeth all men everywhere to repent (Acts 17:30).

The Lord is...not willing that any should perish, but that all should come to repentance (II Peter 3:9).

The apostles taught the necessity of water baptism:

Can any man forbid water, that these should not be

baptized, which have received the Holy Ghost as well as we? And he commanded them to be baptized in the name of the Lord... (Acts 10:47-48).

Then said Paul, John verily baptized with the baptism of repentance, saying unto the people, that they should believe on him which should come after him, that is, on Christ Jesus. When they heard this, they were baptized in the name of the Lord Jesus (Acts 19:5-6).

And now why tarriest thou? arise, and be baptized, and wash away thy sins... (Acts 22:16).

Know ye not, that so many of us as were baptized into Jesus Christ were baptized into his death?.... that like as Christ was raised up from the dead by the glory of the Father, even so we also should walk in newness of life (Romans 6:3-4).

For as many of you as have been baptized into Christ have put on Christ (Galatians 3:27).

Not by works of righteousness which we have done, but according to his mercy he saved us, by the washing of regeneration, and renewing of the Holy Ghost (Titus 3:5).

...while the ark was a preparing, wherein few, that is, eight souls were saved by water. The like figure whereunto even baptism doth also now save us (not the putting away of the filth of the flesh, but the answer of a good conscience toward God,) by the resurrection of Jesus Christ (I Peter 3:20-21).

The apostles taught the necessity of receiving the Holy Ghost (see Titus 3:5 above):

So then they that are in the flesh cannot please God. But ye are not in the flesh, but in the Spirit, if so be that the Spirit of God dwell in you. Now if any man have not the Spirit of Christ, he is none of his (Romans 8:8-9).

The apostles didn't make up this doctrine. They were authorized and empowered by the Spirit of God to continue teaching the same things that Jesus taught.

Acts 2:38 is a very important passage of Scripture because it puts in a "capsule" form the teachings of Jesus and His apostles concerning salvation. It is very important for some other reasons as well. For one, the apostle Peter was given the keys to the kingdom of heaven (see Matthew 16:17-19). In Acts 2:38 he declares what those keys are. Also, Acts 2:38 is a direct response to a direct question, "What shall we do?"

Then Peter said unto them, Repent, and be baptized every one of you in the name of Jesus Christ for the remission of sins, and ye shall receive the gift of the Holy Ghost (Acts 2:38).

Our doctrine should not differ from that of the apostles. To be in God's church we must obey these stipulations. Those that reject God will not obey these fundamental commandments, therefore the unbelievers and the disobedient will not be numbered among the congregation of the righteous (church).

Know ye not that the unrighteous shall not inherit the kingdom of God? Be not deceived: neither fornicators, nor idolaters, nor adulterers, nor effeminate, nor abusers of themselves with mankind, nor thieves, nor covetous, nor drunkards, nor revilers, nor extortioners, shall inherit the kingdom of God. And such were some of you: but ye are washed, but ye are sanctified, but ye are justified in the name of the Lord Jesus, and by the Spirit of our God (I Corinthians 6:9-11).

David declares that the Lord knows the way of the righteous. This means more than just a mental acknowledgment or awareness; it means that He is concerned and involved in the lives of the righteous. The blessed man has the promise that God is personally interested in every detail and concern of his life. He knows the sacrifices and He knows the labors that are done on behalf of His kingdom. He knows when you kept your temper under control and didn't say what you felt like saying. He knows when you give financially in order to see the kingdom progress. He knows your selfless decisions and acts of kindness even when no one else knows at all.

Occasionally we can feel like all these things are to no avail if we don't receive some kind of public recognition. If there's not a tangible physical or material reward we can sometimes get discouraged. But it's a promise that has to be accepted by faith. He knows our heart and sincerity. He knows.

For God is not unrighteous to forget your work and labour of love, which ye have shewed toward his name, in that ye have ministered to the saints, and do minister (Hebrews 6:10).

Because of faithfulness and sincerity of heart the blessed man will prosper. It's a promise. When the majority of Judah was backslidden and rebellious, there was still a remnant that remained faithful and God determined to remember them and reward them:

Then they that feared the Lord spake often one to another: and the Lord hearkened, and heard it, and a book of remembrance was written before him for them that feared the Lord, and that thought upon his name. And they shall be mine, saith the Lord of hosts, in that day when I make up my jewels; and I will spare them, as a man spareth his own son that serveth him (Malachi 3:16-17).

God is also mindful of the deeds and the schemes of the ungodly. The way of the ungodly shall perish.

He that overcometh shall inherit all things; and I will be his God, and he shall be my son. But the fearful, and unbelieving, and the abominable, and murderers, and whoremongers, and sorcerers, and idolaters, and all liars, shall have their part in the lake which burneth with fire and brimstone: which is the second death (Revelation 21:7-8).

In 1984 I graduated high school from Stockton Christian School in Stockton, California. Eighteen years later I was invited to be the commencement speaker at the graduation service for the class of 2002. At the conclusion of this chapter I wish to share with you a story that I shared with them:

In high school I was never the outstanding scholar. My brother was. I was never the outstanding athlete. My brother was. But in 1984 I got this brilliant idea! I made up my mind that I would win "most laps" of Jog-a-thon 1984. Jog-a-thon was (and still is) an important fundraiser for S.C.S. I was determined to win most laps. So I started training. I ran nearly every night through the streets of my neighborhood for several weeks. I would skip rope until I could barely stand up. I was improving my endurance and there was noticeable change. I only told my closest friends what I was doing because I wanted to shock the entire school. I couldn't wait for that chapel service when they would announce my name. When I would receive the trophy. When I would receive the blue ribbon. My name would be placed on a plaque in the office permanently memorializing me with all the other winners before me and those that would follow. On the day of the run I devised a strategy: I would maintain one consistent rate of speed for one hour. So I started running. Nonstop. Lap after lap. It was an extreme test of self-discipline. It was a hot day, but I kept on running. I was sweating, but I kept on running. My legs were trembling, but I kept on running. I could see the plaque in my mind. I ran and I ran and I ran. Thirty-four laps! Finally that special chapel service came. And at the very end they finally announced, "Most laps Jog-a-thon 1984...Darin Bowler." I can still remember the applause. I remember receiving the trophy and the blue ribbon. I won most laps Jog-a-thon 1984! Sadly, however, I failed to get any sponsors for Jog-a-thon 1984. I did not bring in one red cent! In fact, I was a detriment and an expense because they had to buy me a trophy! They had to buy me the blue ribbon! They had to pay to put my name on that plaque! I ran well. I ran hard. I ran fast. But I ran for the wrong reason.

The point is, we may strive, accomplish and attain great things in this life. But don't run for the wrong reason. When all is said and done it will be worth it all to obey and serve God. May YOU be blessed. Amen.

ENDNOTES

Chapter One

1. *Emmett C. Murphy and Michael Snell, The Genius of Sitting Bull (New Jersey:Prentice-Hall,1993)*

Chapter Seven

1.*Illustrations Unlimited, James S. Hewett (Tyndale House Publishers, Inc. ,Wheaton, Illinois) page 302*

ISBN 1-41206008-7

9 781412 060080